When the Great Wheel turns
Who can stand against it?
The rigid break apart,
Therefore, relax and merge.

Yang flows into Yin and becomes empty;
Yin filled, becomes Yang.

Energy flows to the opposite pole,
Thus wealth flows to the simple
And the rich man's money goes out with the tide.

The true healer honors life.
Using the silent language of the heart
She does not speak, yet is understood,
Not promoting herself, people are drawn to her,
Not seeking safety, she is secure,
By serving others, is served by all,
By being ordinary, rises to perfection.

It is true:
Live on the fine edge between light and shadow
And infinite creation is yours.

The cloud does not insist upon its form,
The wave does not force its way over the ocean,
So why should you clutch so tightly
Your little map?

Follow your heart
And know joy in all things.
The path of freedom
Has no markers,
Yet leads to fulfillment;
The path of confusion
Is crowded with signs,
Pointing in all directions.

The Great Way is a humble, solitary path
Leading home;
Follow it closely and be guided.
How do you know you are on the Way?

When your map no longer serves you.

Try to stand above others
And end up on your knees.
Try to get ahead of others
And fall behind yourself.
Trying to prove yourself to others
Means you don't know who you are.
Present a facade to the world,
And you'll live to see it crumble.
Boasting of cures heals no one,
While proclaiming special powers
Will fool some and annoy others.

Spiritual arrogance is a heavy burden indeed;
It looks light, but is hard to bear.
Being honest is much easier
And less annoying.

No matter how great you pretend to be,
It is not as great as you truly are.

If you rely on the power of another
You weaken your own.
If you seek to own the world
You limit your abundance.

The expert guide leads people forward
By plopping them on their rumps,
Dropping the contents of their minds
Down to their bellies.
Removing their goals
Strengthens their intentions.

With a clear mind
They see the confusion desire creates.

Be still and let it happen.

The bird who learns to fly
Must also learn to land.
She flies far
But never forgets her nesting place.

She travels far
Yet understands her boundaries.
She appreciates external beauty
But does not compare herself to it.

The healer is like this.
She channels great joy
And avoids putting on airs;
She visits distant realms
And knows contentment's at home.

One who flits about seeking peace
Forgets to look in her own tree.

The forgiving person carries no burdens,
Walks with a light step;
One who has no attachments perceives perfection
Even in the burning of her own house.

See the smoke?
Everything moves toward God.

Those who live without judgment
Have unshackled their souls
And know the unmeasured tally of eternal suns.
The compassionate person loves Self:
Each deed a graceful act of unthinking kindness.

The lover naturally sees each person as lovable
And in the untouchable an opportunity to embrace.

The fearful judge healer and wounded alike,
But each one wounded has the heart of a healer
And each healer has known a wounded heart.
The liberated soul sees disease
As another remarkable journey.

Fear not, friend:
There is something to be gained
From every illusion.

Firmness is incomplete
Without softness to receive it.
Embrace these two,
And a child is formed,
Perfect, innocent, and free.

Give to the day
Receive from the night;
Honor these two,
Become the ritual of life.

Live your highest aspirations
In an unassuming way:
Cupped hands at the crystal spring.

Be the lump of clay
And the sculptor too:
A universe of unlimited potential.

The universe conforms
To no one's design
Nor can you heal someone
Against their will.

Their purposes are sacred,
Inviolate, encompass realms
Even illumined masters
Dare not tread.
Some are here to celebrate
Others to mourn;
Some here to be sick,
Others to be healed;
Some are here to live,
Others to die;
Some are here to love,
Others to be loved.

One who understands makes no attempt
To solve the puzzle of another,
To stop their world from turning
To keep a soul from learning.

The healer knows
We heal no one
We cure no one;
To attempt a cure
Denies the truth:
Disharmony sown in spirit
Reaps imbalance in the flesh.

To regain the point of balance
Only open your heart,
Merely offer your life;
Allow the Love to heal,
Allow the weak to grow;
Say "I am the healer,"
You step out of the flow.

For the Universe flatters no one,
But merely offers its Life
When you offer your own.

31

Machines are not healers
When they help us forget our higher nature.

Fear aborts intuition,
Birthing a mechanical god.
Can machine repair spirit,
Monitor the presence of love?
Can it hold the hand of a man on the brink
And usher his soul into peace?

Fear of death is the only illness,
The harbinger of quackery and greed.
Those who attack plague as an enemy force
Wield swords of ignorance, arrows of despair;
Rejoice the defeat of each disease,
Wonder the coming of five more;
They applaud the saving of a body,
Oblivious to the soundless *exeunt* of the soul.

True healers spend little time on symptoms,
Rejoice only the opening of a heart.

The Way of Love is infinitely large
And infinitely small.
Bring its light into your world
And watch everything
Fall smoothly into place;
The Mother and Father of All Things
Would conspire on your behalf:
A gentle rain
Of unstrained mercy and joy.

The Mother and Father of All Things
When labeled, judged, divided, structured,
Become prisoners
Locked in little minds.
They agree to imprisonment
They agree to enlightenment
They always say *Yes*.

It is the *Yes* of coming Home
To an open door
A warm hearth.

33

It is wise to yield to another,
Divine to yield to the One within.

A great thing indeed to be the ruler of nations,
Greater still to be the gentle master of your own being.
Inner peace is true abundance,
The poor in spirit seek mere authority.

Be centered and know eternal flow:
Not to save your life,
But to savor it.

Daily, without toil
Mother Earth offers her bountiful harvest.
Life springs from every nook and cranny,
Feeds and animates all
Regardless of religion or reputation.

All we have
All we are
From All That Is.
A gift.

One without wonder
Will not see It
While the eyes of the grateful
Will reflect It.

Peer behind the curtain of time
Part the thin veil of illusion
Travel to the kingdom
Beyond good and evil;
The journey of no distance.

Tempting, colorful, dramatic
The carnival of earthly play;
Drab by comparison
A discussion of the Way.

Unseen, unheard, unlimited.
A pageless book:
The story of us all.

To build up
Dismantle first
To expand
Contract first
To attain clarity
Allow confusion
To become civilized
First live in the wild.

The balance of all things
Is in their opposites;
The truth points in both directions.
Thus the clenched fist holds weakness within
And the open hand offers the hidden power of suns.

Deny one-half yourself,
Stand precariously on one foot.

Love does not enter unless invited
So never meets resistance;
Creative energy flows naturally
From a state of rest;
Thus the Spirit of Love penetrates all
In its motionless embrace.
Earthly creators, reflecting this
Watch each dream come true.

Strong desire creates rigid structure,
The abode of our painful separation.
Accepting the pain of separation
Dissolves the illusion of God's rejection.

The ignorant claim secret knowledge
Hoard it in a sealed chest
And suffocate.
Knowing his heart
To be his source of power
The healer shares it,
Unfolding the rose.

Outwardly, a healer does nothing.
Inwardly, a physician does nothing.
By withdrawing, the healer unifies;
Through intervention, the physician divides.
The less one does, the less there is to do.
The more one does, the more one needs to do,
And original error multiplies.

The healer offers love and empowers the soul.
The physician offers concern and treats the body.
The orderly glares at the patient and enforces
    procedure.
Thus, when love is denied
Concern is dispensed
When concern is denied
Procedures must be followed to the letter.

Procedures alone are a mouthful of chaff,
Impossible to swallow.
Prognosis comes next, attempts to dictate the Tao

And deny the miraculous.
What folly!

Therefore, the healer parts the shade
And reveals the light,
Sees past the pain and into the heart,
Reaches through the chaff to cradle the blossom.

Life is eternal and everywhere
Yet remains a quality precious,
Treasured and rare.

Receive the quality of openness and know clarity,
Centeredness, and know focus,
Playfulness, and know joy;
Receive the quality of humility
And know the greatness of Life.

Without openness there is separation
Without centeredness, interference
Without playfulness, decay
Without humility, the endless repetition of pain.

Humility is the highest blessing of Life;
Through it the great serve the lowly
And the lowly serve the great.
In this way the Universe ever uplifts itself:
The endless nativity of Light.

Returning to Wholeness is the natural way;
Allow, allow, allow.

The choice to Love
Is the Mother of Everything.
There are no exceptions.

Those who know Love
Know its facility in all matters;
Others find it useful occasionally
While the broken-hearted bitterly laugh
And deny Love altogether.
Can you hear in their laughter
The sound of Heaven?

God is not to blame for the separation.
He has never turned His back on you.
Blame is the disease
Which blinds you to unity's truth.

Wake up; the nightmare is over.
The light is in them
As well as in you.
The thinnest of veils
Divides the two.
You are one Self.

You are not weak, but strong.
You are not limited, but unlimited.
You are not unloved, but much beloved.
You have suffered only for this:
That you may bless those who suffer still.

In the beginning, a Voice whispered
"I Love You . . . pass it on."

And so the seamless became sectioned
Each embracing the other
Each containing seed of the other
And the One.

Thus we live, each seeking balance
A remembrance of Harmony
Amongst all creation.

Eons of worldly pain
The desolate march
The vale of tears
The pall of forgetfulness
Merely the Mother's bittersweet
Moment of labor:

The foreplay of unspeakable joy.

To penetrate the hardest armor,
Use the softest touch.
Yielding melts resistance
Density is filled by light
Good work accomplished without effort.

In silence the teachings are heard;
In stillness the world is transformed.

Would you rather be known by others
Or know your self?
Is making money more important
Than freedom?
Is security sought more than service?

The greedy get the least
The stingy lose the most
The fearful fare the poorest.
The one willing to give all away for free
Only grows richer.
The one who gives his life to love
Has nothing to lose.

"If it isn't broken, don't fix it."
The Universe isn't broken
And neither are You.
So don't attempt to fix others
Until you realize that you yourself are perfect.

The lame man's crutches
Are as much a part of him
As the wind
The birds
The sea.

Meditate on this
And watch the complicated grow simple.

If you're hungry, eat.
If you're tired, rest.
Stop tampering with Life
And enjoy the ride.

Will peace be found
In the sound of a dropping bomb
In the city center,
Or in the gentle plop
Of horse droppings
On a farmer's field?

Fear breeds greed
Greed, control
Control, discontent.
Disaster is the result.

Feed yourself and never have enough;
Feed others and never go hungry.

The beauty of all existence
Rests within you:
Heaven peers from your two eyes.
Compare yourself to another,
Watch how quickly the light goes out.

Thus, when you see beauty within
You'll see it without;
As heaven shows
The healer knows.
Unconditional love has no opposite.
This is true balance.

Science constantly adds to medical knowledge.
It gets so complicated, who can understand it all?
Love is very simple,
It requires no thought or deed in order to work.

Anyone can do it.
Master the art of letting love happen.

Love flows into a clear mind
Ripples outward to those in need.

Your kind deeds, your loving thoughts
Travel invisible pathways,
Elevate rulers and ruled alike
A world, even worlds away.
Likewise, your faith
May light a thousand cities
Endowing both the kindly and the cruel.

Strength in one is strength in all
And light in one brings light to all.
The truth about yourself is healing.
Don't hold anything back.

Lose focus on life
And enter death's realm.
The body,
Full of holes
Where deadly plagues may enter;
Arms and legs,
Subject to the sword;
The erring ego held fast to the wheel
Death after death.

The illusion is this.
There is no ego,
There is only the fear the ego creates.
You cannot fear death,
For fear *is* death.
You cannot choose between
Life and death,
For there is only life.

One who walks permeated with life
Fears neither plague nor sword nor sin,
Sees death as the artifice of man.

We spring forth from the All,
Fed by light,
Clothed in matter,
Sculpted by streams of inspiration,
We shape Love like the eagle shapes the wind.
Returning at last to the Sun,
We bring only our joy of flight.

When the Mothering Spirit gives birth,
Her light effortlessly feeds, shelters,
Nurtures, and uplifts.
So the true healer
Nurtures but does not control
Shelters but does not imprison
Guides others to the edge of the cliff
But does not force them to fly.

One Mother, many women.
One Father, many men.
One Spirit, many bodies.

Love the Mother in your self,
She's found in the eyes of all creation.
See Her in others,
And you'll know Her, your Self,
The triviality of death.

In life, be a listener.
Keep an even temper,
Avoid boastful displays.
Respect yourself and be tolerant of others.
Don't try to control or merge
With everything you see.
This brings tranquility, stability, and harmony.

In the small things,
See the Mother's touch.
Remember that Nature prefers adaptation
To domination.
Seek your inner light,
And trust it to guide you Home.

It's actually much easier
And more fun
To be compassionate, kind,
Generous and forgiving.
But people seem to forget this
And wonder why they find themselves
In a world out of balance.

When we forget ourselves
We lose touch with the Earth,
Believe in powerlessness,
Invent a wrathful God
Cruel leaders
Uncaring parents
Rebellious children
A desolate world.

Your relationship with the Universe
Reflects what you remember.
There is no advantage to living in fear:
Wake up and pay attention.

A simple selfless act is a gift
Remembered by generations of children.

You are the source of Love.
Love your children as yourself
And live to see this light
Shine upon cities, nations, planets, stars.

There is no limit to what you can do.

The healer allows Love's harmonious flow

Like an infant child
Soft, receiving, trusting.
But what a tenacious grip
On Mother's breast!

The babe knows nothing of sex
Yet its energy flows through the body
Shamelessly, sensitive and alive
To each pleasing moment.
Its screams and cries
Come straight from the Source
It can cry all day and not get hoarse.

The healer is like this:
Unjudging, unafraid of Love's presence
Whatever form it takes.
Unflattered by power
Unhindered by shame
Unfettered by rules.

So childishly immortal:
Only the grown-up believes in death.

Those who know, are silent;
Those who do not, babble on forever.

Surrender your demands
Forego your dramas
Ignore magical tricks
Abandon the marketplace
Claim neither victory nor defeat;
Feel Earth living in muscle and blood.

Spoken, it loses meaning.
Lived, its power transcends limitation.

First, be kind and loving to yourself
As you would love a child;
Allow spontaneity and play in your work
And know the effortless healing
Of God's indiscriminate laughter.

Remember, the more complicated the system
The more confused the client;
The more difficult the treatment
The less likely the cure;
The more secret the method
The more scarce the love.

Remain quiet within
And they will resonate with peace;
Sow silence, and they'll reap wisdom;
Step aside, and they will heal themselves.

Let go your desire to heal:
Watch God emerge.

58

Love's rule is One,
Man's rules are many.
Delusion and pain are a tangle of rules
While peace has no limitation.

When fear speaks
Happiness becomes pain
And desperately people cling
To straws of sorrow.
Their left hands use magic
To repel dark spirits,
And with their fright
They invite them in again.

What is pain
But love unexpressed?
Be unshakable
But not obstinate;
Embrace fear
But do not affirm it;
Feel pain
But do not believe it.

When channeling the forces of heaven
The boundaries of your being create flow,
As canyon walls transform lakes into rivers.

The soul free from dogma
Permits an unobstructed stream:
The freer the soul, the freer the flow.

Thus, use your limits as allies
That you may produce unlimited results;
Be open as the Mother
That the Father may enter;
To impart Heaven, be a vessel of earth.

60

Lay on hands as you would touch a young child;
When the energy flows between you,
Why push hard to go deep?
When Love fills you,
Why be concerned with evil?
Dark spirits have no hold on the humble
And the loving healer is uplifted
By each encounter.

To give, receive.
Be the wet, fertile valley
That rivers of life flow through.
The full will be emptied
The empty, filled.
So be empty, that you may be filled.

The greatest healer shares all
And becomes yet greater.
One who wants to be healed
Must become a healer.
And one who wants to be a healer
Must first seek healing;
Suffering gains meaning only when healed
And healing is meaningless
Until it is shared.

To receive, give.

Words can be cheap, deeds hollow;
But when filled with truth
Reflect the glory of the One:
Irresistible pathways of focused light.

Thus when one asks to be your student
Don't waste your time on theory or style.
Teach them to respond like a master,
Love like a child.
From this the rest will follow.

Why is this way great?
Because when you ask, you receive
When you seek, you find
When you err, you're forgiven;
Endlessly and forever
No one's condemned or excluded.

Take heart!

In action find stillness.
Seek the simple kernel
At the heart of every matter.
See the greatness in a small, kindly gesture.
Make forgiveness your intention
And your enemies are allies:
Love is perceived in all you meet.

Civilized man, afraid of Nature's simplicity
Creates complex problems;
The healer creates wholeness
By loving whomever God has put in his way.

When there is trust, promises are not required
And the difficult challenge is met with joy.

Health is easy to keep,
Difficult to restore;
Emotions move easily
When first they arise,
Become pain when suppressed;
To respond and release
Means less toil later.

An armored heart is easily injured
And pursuing fantasy invites despair;
A great life is composed of many details,
So walk firmly — each step counts.

A grand canyon began as a tiny cleft
A great master was born a small babe;
Be happy in your place,
Growth is inevitable.
Your start and finish are the same:
The journey to enlightenment begins
Where you are right now.

One who controls
Will be out of control
And the competitive spirit
Is ever wanting.
The sage does not control
And maintains perfect balance;

She does not grab for power
So overflows with it.

The only treasure the master seeks
Is a peaceful heart;
Her only goal
To be fully where she is.
Her only doctrine
To allow.

By returning to her origins,
She brings us all forward.

The World Teachers never etched their words
On paper or stone
For all to obey;
They knew people would only split hairs, bicker,
Compel others to follow their folly.

The more you listen to preachers,
The more you'll moralize and judge,
So go learn on your own.

Everything is written inside:
You are The Book.

Go back.
Uplift the fallen child.

There's no need to pretend any more.
She's hurt and afraid and needs your help.
Set your desires aside for one moment
And see clearly what needs to be done.

You expect a child to take care of you?
Let him go and let his imagination
Teach you both.

There's no need to hide.
Declare your needs honestly
And watch the world scramble to assist.
Invite them in to join the celebration!

Some say that living in the moment is absurd and
   irresponsible.
How can you trust those who might harm you?
How will you survive without planning and toil?
How can you heal without first being schooled?
Fear of death,
Fear of want,
The fear of separation from God.

To choose to trust allows the fullest expression of life.
To choose to serve creates the greatest abundance.
To choose compassion brings Oneness and health.
Values found only moment by moment
Banishing all fear.
The only rational response to life.

The true healer does not rush to judgment,
Or try to conquer disease;
He knows that simply being available
Is his greatest gift.

Not ruled by guilt,
He's not out to save the world
Or tell others how to live.

The healer opens the gates of heaven for others
For simple reasons:
Because he likes people
And it feels good.

The precipice of vanity
Is obscured by certainty;
Tread humbly, be willing to retreat.
A confused mind is easily cleared;
Step backward, return to light.

Anger stands its ground
Insists on being right,
And the fearful maneuver
Always to save face.
Engage these and discover the tiresome futility
Of conversation with a mask.

View all through the clear lens of compassion
Find the Healer behind each disguise.

It is simple to feel
Yet few feel it.

It is the feeling of ancient origin
The emotion that births creation;
Available to all
Expressed by few.

The arrogant see it
Yet do not know it
And deride it,
This diamond spark that dwells
In a crude vessel of clay.

Some prefer knowing to being.
Their illness is in their heads.
Some prefer being to knowing.
Their illness is in their hearts.

She who knows her illness is in her heart
Is halfway home.

Denying his broken heart
No longer awed or inspired
The cynic courts disaster.
So save your high convincing talk:
He won't hear it;
In your most skilled technique
He'll find flaws.

Love all he says and all he does
Honor his arrogance and his pain
Hold him in the highest light
And fill his greatest need.

One man kills for peace
Another lives for it;
Yet the first man loves his dog
And beats his children,
And the other loves his children
And beats his dog.
Would you be so bold to declare
Which man Heaven loves most?

Love's flame glows
In both victor and vanquished.
Who has won?
Who has lost?
God lives in both master and slave.
Who is beating whom?

It's been written, "All that has happened,
Has had to happen.
All that must happen
Will happen."
So who can stand outside the circle of Heaven
To direct its grasp?

Look around you.
Fear of death
Is not reverence for life,
And fear of illness
Will not bring health.

Can you choose wisely
Can you see deeply
Can you touch deftly enough
To unravel this karmic knot?
Step aside and let Heaven loose,
Lest you yourself become caught
And strangle in the tangle.

Spirit and body go hungry
When outcome takes precedence over love.
Forget your intention to Wholeness:
Congestion in the flow.

Be willing to trust
And soar high on the mountain.
Live only for your accomplishments
And hang by the edge of the cliff
Once again.

The young initiate is a willing new bud;
The jaded expert, a thicket of brittle thorns.
Seek new ways, and the path will never end;
Be certain of your knowledge
And death's around the bend.

When disease emerges
Accept, embrace, listen, respond.
Receive the blessing of those who suffer;
They are the heroes
Who show us the divine in ourselves.
Return the favor!

When healing is the target
Illness is the bow.
What is a bow but a device for the transfer of energy?
Likewise an illness.

Properly used, an illness turns an outward focus
     inward,
Sends energy to where it's needed most.
Transforms fears into strength
Arrogance into humility
Compulsion to caring
Cynicism to compassion
Brings balance to imbalance.

The release of pain over-long denied.

Worldly medicine does the opposite.
It requires the patient to look outside herself
To give her power to another
To maintain control
To invade the body
To deny the spirit.

One who embraces illness as well as health
Embraces the whole of life.
She can offer life
Because she receives life.

What is more feminine than water?
It is soft and yielding,
Yet nothing impedes
Its homeward flow to the Ocean,
And cliffs fall
Under water's constant caress.

This is obvious to all
But will you apply it to your life?

Master softness,
Don't push against the obstacle;
Yield and flow
Yield and flow.

Attack disease and invite battle;
Surrender to Love
And know true victory.

Like water, truth embraces
Both stone and starlight.

If someone removes symptoms,
Proclaims "You are healed!"
But imbalance remains, what good is that?
Better to say, "I forgive you,"
And get to the heart of the matter.
A true healer takes the challenging way,
Feeling all, accepting all, releasing all;
So becoming whole.

The Spirit of Love is impartial,
Yet only comes to those who ask.

A simple person leading a simple life
Knows true riches;
Living her purpose,
She's not compelled to devise a complicated
And gaudy life.
At peace with her many facets,
She feels no need to wander about,
Searching for what's inside.
At home with the secrets of life,
She practically ignores them
Preferring to take life as it comes.

Delighting in a kind gesture,
A quiet moment with a friend,
She knows her sphere of influence
And fills it with light.

With the gates of heaven in her hands
She prefers to live and die right here;
For, in all the universe,
Here is where she serves.

Master, where will you seek truth,
In these flowery phrases
Or in the quiet solace of your own heart?
Even the ego pretends to be wise,
And whispers sage counsel in God's name.
Fearing death, it can never perceive the light.

Embrace death and receive life:
In the infinite sphere all is possible
So what is there to debate?
Living through eternity
What experience will you miss?
Having the universe at your disposal
What is there to possess?

Only the courageous surrender enough
To receive all the Universe has to offer.

New World Library is dedicated to
publishing books and cassettes that inspire
and challenge us to improve the quality
of our lives and our world.

Our books and cassettes are available
in bookstores everywhere.
For a catalog of our complete library
of fine books and cassettes, contact:

New World Library
14 Pamaron Way
Novato, CA 94949

Telephone: (415) 884-2100
Fax: (415) 884-2199
Or call toll-free (800) 972-6657
Catalog requests: Ext. 50
Ordering: Ext. 52

E-mail: escort@nwlib.com
http://www.nwlib.com